Jesus and the Woman at the Well

John 4:1–42 for children

Written by Melinda Busch
Illustrated by Bill Clark

Arch® Books
Copyright © 2004 Concordia Publishing House
3558 S. Jefferson Avenue, St. Louis, MO 63118-3968
Manufactured in Columbia

Jesus and His followers
Had stopped along their way,
While traveling through Samaria
That hot and dusty day.

The disciples left the Master
To sit and rest a spell.
They went on to buy some food;
He sat down near a well.

A sad and weary woman
Who thought she was the worst
Came to Jacob's ancient well
Where waters quench the thirst.

She knew her heart was dirty
And broken with her sin,
But though she longed for cleansing,
She had no hope within.

"Please give me some," He asked her,
In kind and gentle tone.
She turned to face Him, startled;
She thought she was alone.

"Why would you, a Jewish man,
Ask me for a drink?
I am a Samaritan!"
She knew not what to think.

The Savior answered softly,
His voice was kind and true,
"If you knew the gift of God
And who stood here with you,

"You would have asked from Him
Water that is living,
And He would have offered it
With pleasure at the giving."

The woman looked at Jesus,
Her heart began to leap.
"But Sir, You have no bucket,
The well is very deep.

"Where is this living water?
Who are You? Please do tell.
Are You greater than Jacob,
The one who dug this well?"

"The water of this well is good,"
Said Jesus with a smile.
"But drink it now and you will see,
You'll need more in a while.

"The water that I offer,
You neither see nor swallow,
It's for the soul instead of lips—
You need only follow."

"But Sir, I am a sinner.
Can God still want me now?"
"I know, my child, what you've done.
I forgive you anyhow."

She said, "You are a prophet.
When will Messiah come,
Who will tell us everything?"
He said, "I am that One."

The woman left her water jar
And ran into the town
To spread the news of Jesus
To everyone around.

They hurried to see Jesus
And begged Him not to leave.
Many more believed in Him—
Forgiveness they received.

And though your heart be sinful,
Christ forgives you too,
Through water, bread, and wine,
And through His Word of truth.

Dear Parents,

Most of us take water for granted. It's a necessary part of every single day, yet we seldom think about it. We open a bottle and drink it, hop in the tub and wash in it, turn on a faucet and cook with it. It's there almost every time we need it or want it.

Read this Bible story in John 4:1–42. The woman at the well had made some bad choices in a long search to fill a void in her life. She was thirsty for fulfillment—for love—that is not found in ordinary things. Jesus knew that and He reached out.

He told the woman, "Whoever drinks the water I give him will never thirst. Indeed the water I give him will become in him a spring of water welling up to eternal life" (John 4:14). The living water Jesus offered filled her life as nothing else had. Overjoyed, she spread the word in her parched, pagan village. Many people were quenched by the Lord's forgiveness and promise of salvation.

Just as Jesus, God the Son, knew the sinful woman's heart, He knows what is in our hearts too. Only Jesus gives us the one thing that will satisfy the thirst caused by our sin—forgiveness. In the water and Word of Baptism, in the cup and the bread of the Lord's Supper, God washes away our sin and refreshes us with His grace. He offers it freely.

As Christ's living water fills the void, it also bubbles up and overflows. The more we drink of it, the more there is, and, like the woman at the well, the more we want to share it with others!